MY FIRST LOOK AT COMMUNITIES

TOWNS HAVE MANY DIFFERENT KINDS OF BUILDINGS

A Town

VALERIE BODDEN

SAUNDERS
BOOK COMPANY

Paperback edition published in 2010 by Saunders Book Company
27 Stewart Road, Collingwood, ON Canada L9Y 4M7

Designed by Rita Marshall

Photographs by Getty Images (Johner Images, National Geographic, Photographer's
Choice, Photonica, Stone, Taxi, The Image Bank, Visuals Unlimited)

Copyright © 2008 Creative Education
Creative Education is an imprint of The Creative Company
P.O. Box 227, Mankato, Minnesota 56002

Printed in the United States of America

Library and Archives Canada Cataloguing in Publication

Bodden, Valerie
    A town / Valerie Bodden.

(My first look at communities)
Includes bibliographical references.
ISBN 978-1-926722-32-0

    I. City and town life—Juvenile literature. I. Title. II.
Series: My first look at communities (Collingwood, Ont.).

HT I52.B67 2009   j307.76'3   C2009-902944-8

A Town

Smaller than a City

A town is a lot like a city. But most towns are smaller than cities. They do not have as many buildings as cities do.

Most of the buildings in towns are smaller than the buildings in cities. There are not usually any **skyscrapers**. But there are houses, stores, and churches.

STORES IN TOWNS CAN BE BUSY PLACES

Not as many people live in a town as in a city. Most towns are not as busy as cities, either. But there can still be a lot going on in towns. Cars drive down the streets. Kids play on playgrounds. Grown-ups shop in stores. Families go for long walks.

LIVING IN A TOWN

People all around the world live in towns. Some people in towns live in **apartments**. But most people in towns live in houses. Most of the houses have yards.

Some towns have a curfew.

This means that kids cannot be

on the streets after a certain time.

SOME TOWNS ARE SPREAD ACROSS A WIDE AREA

Many people work in towns. Some work in stores. Others work in offices. Some work in **factories**. Some people who live in towns drive to a city to work.

Most towns have a school for kids. Some small towns do not have a school. Kids who live in those towns have to ride a bus to another town or city for school.

There are some old towns

that no one lives in anymore.

These are called ghost towns.

Animals in a Town

Animals live in towns, too. Some of them live with people. They are pets. Many people in towns keep dogs and cats as pets. Some people keep rabbits as pets. Other people keep hamsters.

Other animals in towns are not pets. They are **wild**. Squirrels and some rabbits are wild. They live in towns. Raccoons are wild. They

In some towns, garbage collectors
pick up people's garbage. Sometimes
raccoons get to it first!

RACCOONS LOOK FOR SNACKS IN PEOPLE'S GARBAGE

live in towns, too. There are lots of wild birds in most towns.

Some towns have rivers or ponds. Fish live in the water. Ducks might swim in the water. Frogs live near the water. So do snakes.

A TOWN'S RIVER IS A GOOD HOME FOR DUCKS

Time for Fun

There are lots of ways to have fun in towns. You can go shopping. Some towns have restaurants to eat at. Some have movie theaters.

Many towns have a park. Kids can play at the park. Some towns are close to the **country**. People can walk or drive to the country. Then they can look at fields or trees. They might even see farm animals such as cows.

Some towns have special

parks for riding skateboards.

The parks have ramps to skate on.

At night, most towns are quiet. Stores close. People go in the house and turn off the lights. Then everyone goes to sleep. They rest so they will be ready for another day of work and play in the town!

A TOWN IS A PEACEFUL PLACE TO LIVE

Hands-on: Make a School Bus

Lots of kids in towns ride a school bus. You can make your own bus!

What You Need

An egg carton lid

A milk jug lid

Yellow tempera paint

Black construction paper

A paintbrush

A pencil

A black marker

Glue

What You Do

1. Paint the egg carton lid yellow.
2. After the paint dries, write the word "SCHOOL" on the lid.
3. Use the milk jug lid to trace two circles on the black construction paper. Have a grown-up help you cut them out and glue them near the bottom of the egg carton lid for wheels.
4. Imagine all the kids on your bus!

KIDS WHO LIVE FAR FROM SCHOOL RIDE THE BUS

Index

Words to Know

apartments—sets of rooms inside a bigger building with many others that look the same

country—an area with lots of land but not many houses or other buildings

factories—places where people make things such as cars, toasters, or crayons

skyscrapers—very tall buildings that look like they can touch the sky

wild—an animal that is not a pet

Read More

Caseley, Judith. *On the Town: A Community Adventure.* New York: Greenwillow Books, 2002.

Geisert, Bonnie. *River Town.* Boston: Houghton Mifflin, 1999.

Press, Judy. *All Around Town! Exploring Your Community Through Craft Fun.* Charlotte, Vt.: Williamson Publishing, 2002.

Explore the Web

Field Trip http://www.hud.gov/kids/field1.html

KidsTown http://www.jugband.org/kidstown/cgi-bin/kt.cgi?KEY=1000

My Town Is Important http://www.mrsmcgowan.com/town/showcase.htm